Food and Festivals

A Flavour of

ITALY

Saviour Pirotta

HODDER
Wayland

an imprint of Hodder Children's Books

Other titles:

Cover photograph:
An Italian food shop.

Title page: A float at the Viareggio carnival.

Contents page: A young stilt walker at the Venice carnival.

First published in Great Britain in 1999 by Wayland Publishers Limited

First published in paperback in 2002 by Hodder Wayland, an imprint of Hodder Children's Books

© Hodder Wayland 1999

Hodder Children's Books
A division of Hodder Headline Limited
338 Euston Road, London NW1 3BH

Series editor: Polly Goodman
Book editor and picture researcher: Cath Senker
Designer: Tim Mayer
Cover picture research: Paula Chapman

British Library Cataloguing in Publication Data
Pirotta, Saviour
    A Flavour of Italy. – (Food and Festivals)
    1. Cookery, Italian – Juvenile literature
    2. Festivals – Italy – Juvenile literature
    3. Food habits – Italy – Juvenile literature
    4. Italy – Social customs – Juvenile literature
    I. Title
    641.5'945
    ISBN 0 7502 4204 3

Typeset by Mayer Media
Printed and bound in Hong Kong

CONTENTS

Italy and its Food

SWITZERLAND

AUSTRIA

FRANCE

AOSTA VALLEY

PIEDMONT

LOMBARDY

SLOVENIA

ITALY

Verona • • Venice

PO VALLEY

CROATIA

LIGURIA

BOSNIA-HERZEGOVINA

ADRIATIC SEA

Viareggio •

Florence •

N

• Perugia

Lake Bolsena

ABRUZZO

Rome •

MOLISE

PUGLIA

CAMPANIA

SARDINIA

Naples •

• Putignano

• Taranto

0   200 km

0   125 miles

• Cagliari

MEDITERRANEAN SEA

CALABRIA

SICILY

IONIAN SEA

ITALY

Italy's place in the world

WHEAT

Wheat and maize are the most important cereals grown in Italy. Different kinds of wheat are used for making pasta, bread and cakes.

FRUIT

Apples, peaches and citrus fruits are important crops. Every region in Italy has its own vineyards, where grapes are grown for wine.

CHEESE AND MILK

Grated Parmesan cheese is sprinkled on spaghetti, and mozzarella cheese, made from buffalo milk, is used as a topping for pizzas. Milk is also used to make ice-cream.

VEGETABLES

Italy produces many different vegetables. Tomatoes are made into various sauces. Onions, peppers and garlic give food a strong flavour.

OLIVES

Olive trees grow in most parts of Italy. The olives are pressed to make olive oil, one of the most popular ingredients in Italian cooking.

MEAT

Italians eat a lot of fresh meat, such as chicken, beef, veal, lamb and pork. They also enjoy the meat of wild animals, such as rabbits and birds.

Food and Farming

Italy is a long, narrow country in southern Europe. In the northern part of the country there is plenty of rain, and cereals such as wheat and maize grow well. In the south, the weather is much hotter. Lemons, grapes and olives can be grown.

Delicious Italian foods, such as pizza, pasta and ice-cream, are a part of everyday life around the world. Many people forget that these foods come from Italy.

▼ A farmer checks the harvest in an Italian wheat field.

Cereals and rice

Wheat and maize are the most important cereals grown in Italy. Wheat is used for making bread, cakes, pizza and pasta. Italians buy pasta fresh or dried. Some even make their own at home.

Rice is grown in some regions too. The most famous rice comes from the Po Valley. It is cooked with cheese and garlic to make a creamy dish called *risotto*.

▲ Traditional Italian bread is cooked in wood-burning ovens. Many bakeries are run by families.

Cheese and milk

The mountains and fertile plains of northern Italy are good for grazing cows. Many kinds of cheese are made from their milk. The Aosta Valley is known for cheeses such as *robiola* and *fontina*. Nearby in Lombardy, dairy farmers make *mascarpone*, *gorgonzola* and *taleggio*.

Further south, in the region of Abruzzo, farmers raise sheep to make special cheeses such as *pecorino*.

▲ Farmers in the town of Eboli, near Naples, make *mozzarella* cheese from buffalo milk.

▼ Buffaloes in Agropoli, near Naples. Buffalo milk cannot be drunk and is only used to make cheese.

FRUIT AND VEGETABLES

The Italians hold many festivals to celebrate the different fruits and vegetables grown in their country. In the region of Liguria, there are aubergine, lemon, cherry, strawberry and chestnut festivals.

Another chestnut festival is held on the island of Sardinia. The people of Aritzo, a town surrounded by chestnut groves, welcome visitors with boiled and roasted chestnut treats.

Fruit and vegetables

Italy produces grapes, olives and citrus fruits, such as oranges and lemons. Olives grow in most parts of the country. They can be eaten, or pressed to make olive oil.

▲ Farmers from Venice show off their harvest in a gondola, a type of boat.

Italian farmers produce a large variety of crops, depending on the climate. In the southern region of Campania, where the soil is rich and there are long, hot summers, farmers grow plum tomatoes. In other regions asparagus, beans, cauliflowers, onions and garlic are grown.

▲ Women in southern Italy prepare cured meats to be used in cooked dishes, salads and sandwiches.

Meat

Italians enjoy a wide range of meat in their dishes. In the north, farmers keep cows, so people cook a lot of beef and veal. Pigs are raised too. Pork is eaten all over the country, either fresh or cured as sausages and ham. Further south, where the land is drier, farmers keep sheep, poultry, rabbits and goats.

Fish

Most of Italy is surrounded by the Mediterranean and Adriatic Seas. People in coastal towns eat fresh fish and seafood. In the north, people catch fish from lakes, rivers and streams. Anchovies, swordfish, tuna, squid, octopus and whitebait are popular ingredients in Italian cooking.

▼ A fishing boat prepares to leave the harbour of Trapani on the island of Sicily.

FESTIVAL AT SEA

There are many local fish festivals in Italy. The parade at the festival of San Cataldo in Taranto actually takes place on the sea. People at the festival eat fried fish as part of the celebrations.

Family Celebrations

Most Italians are Roman Catholics. Catholicism is a Christian religion, headed by the Pope. Mary, the mother of Jesus, is particularly important to Catholics.

Catholics celebrate the most important events of their lives with special religious ceremonies. Baptisms, weddings and funerals all take place in church. Happy occasions are always followed by a huge party, to which friends and family are invited.

Italians have *feste*, ▶ which are special days to honour saints. These girls are celebrating the festival of Saint Efisio, in Cagliari, Sardinia.

▼ A procession in Puglia to honour Saint Cosmas and Saint Damian.

ALL SAINTS' DAY

All Saints' Day takes place on 1 November. Catholics honour dead people who led a good life. Children eat special biscuits shaped like beans. They are called *fave dolce romane* (sweet Roman beans, or bean-shaped biscuits). There's a recipe for the biscuits on page 17.

Weddings

Italian weddings are very lavish. The long ceremony in church is followed by a meal that can have up to fourteen courses. Meals vary from region to region, but usually start with an elegant *antipasto*, such as Parma ham. This may be followed by soup, a small pasta dish, chicken, rabbit or fish.

Sugared almonds, called *confetti*, are found at every wedding. Sometimes they are arranged so that they look like bunches of flowers, and are put next to the place cards on the table.

◀ Many Italians have their wedding feast out of doors. These people are celebrating in their home town of Calabria.

At some weddings, the *confetti* are wrapped in little bags and handed out by the bridesmaids. Each parcel is called a *bomboniera*. There are five almonds in each *bomboniera*. They stand for health, happiness, wealth, children and a long life.

▲ The wedding cake is usually a light sponge, flavoured with a liqueur and a special filling called *zuppa inglese*. The cake is covered with fresh cream.

Local festivals

▲ Bean-shaped biscuits for All Saints' Day. There's a recipe for these biscuits on page 17.

The Italian calendar is packed with local festivals. Most of them, like the Festival of Saint Dominic in Cocullo, Abruzzo, are held in honour of patron saints. There are processions and fireworks. Snacks and delicious Italian ice-cream are sold on street stalls.

Many festivals celebrate crops and harvests. In the town of Collelongo, Abruzzo, there is a cooking pot festival. The pots are blessed by a local priest and a prize is given to the owner of the best saucepan.

SAINT DOMINIC

Many Italians believe that Saint Dominic protects them from snake bites. During the Festival of Saint Dominic, a statue covered in snakes is paraded around the streets. Five girls follow the statue. They carry a special sweet pastry ring in a basket on their heads. After the festival, the pastry ring is given to the men who took part in the parade.

Everyone from the fishing town ▶ of Marta, on Lake Bolsena, comes to the yearly fish festival. There is a procession of fishermen, and children push wheelbarrows of fruit and vegetables.

Bean-shaped Biscuits

EQUIPMENT

Mixing bowl   Grater
Wooden spoon   Chopping board
Mixing spoon   Knife
Small mixing bowl   Baking tray
Egg beater   Spatula

INGREDIENTS (makes 12)

100 g Plain flour
90 g Butter, softened
50 g Granulated sugar
1 Egg, beaten
50 g Ground almonds
½ Teaspoon powdered cinnamon
Zest of half a lemon, grated
1 Tablespoon icing sugar

1 Put the flour and butter in the mixing bowl and mix with the wooden spoon until smooth.

2 Add the sugar, cinnamon, almonds, beaten egg and lemon zest. Mix together to make a smooth dough. Add a little more flour if it is sticky.

3 Roll the dough into a 15-cm long sausage, and cut into 12 slices. With clean hands, pinch each slice into a broad-bean shape and flatten slightly.

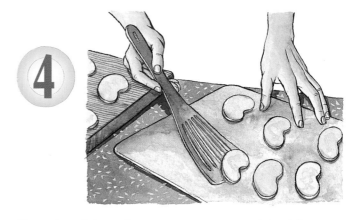

4 Put the biscuits on a greased baking tray. Bake for 15 minutes at 180° C (Gas Mark 4) or until golden brown. When cool, sprinkle with icing sugar.

Always be careful with hot ovens. Ask an adult to help you.

Christmas and New Year

Christmas is the most important festival in Italy. It celebrates the day when Jesus was born. Each house is decorated with a *presepio*, which is a nativity scene filled with little statues. Nativity scenes are also set up in churches and near famous landmarks. In some towns, people dress up as characters from the Christmas story.

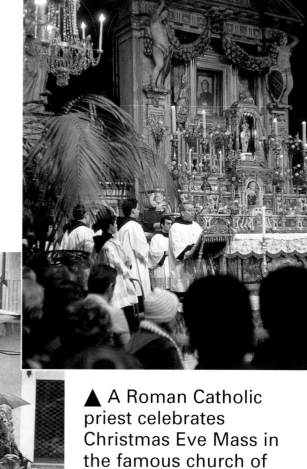

▲ A Roman Catholic priest celebrates Christmas Eve Mass in the famous church of Aracoeli in Rome.

◀ The main figures in a *presepio* are Jesus, Mary and Joseph. There are shepherds and animals around them.

▲ *Panettone,* a traditional Italian cake with dried fruit.

Christmas food

Many Italians fast for twenty-four hours before having a traditional dinner on Christmas Eve. Meals vary from region to region. Some people have fish and seafood stew served with vegetables. Others enjoy lamb, turkey, or spaghetti with anchovies.

Two more big meals are eaten on Christmas Day and New Year's Eve. The New Year's Eve menu might include raisin bread, turkey, rabbit and pasta. People in certain regions eat a special lentil and sausage dish too.

New Year and Epiphany

The Christmas celebrations end on 6 January, the Epiphany. On this day, people remember the three wise men who visited baby Jesus.

Children wait for the Befana, an old woman who brings presents for good children (a bit like Father Christmas). Naughty children are supposed to be given a lump of coal. But the Befana knows that all children are sometimes good and sometimes naughty. She leaves everyone a lump of coal as well as some treats.

NEW YEAR'S EVE

On New Year's Eve, Italians throw old furniture and junk out of the window. This is believed to get rid of bad luck and make way for better times.

▼ Lentils are supposed to bring you more money in the New Year. See the recipe opposite to make this lucky lentil and sausage dish.

Lentils and Sausage

INGREDIENTS (for 4)

250 g Red lentils
1 Tablespoon olive oil
1 Small onion, finely chopped
1 Stalk celery, chopped
½ Medium-sized carrot
2 Tablespoons tomato purée
1 Cup chicken stock
A pinch of dried sage
250 g Salami or pepperoni

EQUIPMENT

Sieve
Saucepan
Frying pan with lid
Chopping board
Knife
Wooden spoon
Ladle

Wash the lentils using a sieve. Cook them in water until soft but firm.

Fry the chopped onion in the oil until soft. Add the chopped celery and carrot. Cook on a low heat with the lid on for 10 minutes.

Drain the lentils and add them to the vegetables in the pan. Stir in the tomato purée, the stock and the sage.

Cook for 3 more minutes, then serve mixed with the salami, sliced into small pieces 1 cm thick.

Always be careful with hot liquids and pans. Ask an adult to help you.

Carnival

▼ A young stilt walker at the Venice carnival.

Carnival is an ancient festival. Before Italy became a Christian country, it was a festival to celebrate the fertility of the land. Today most Catholics see it as a last chance to have fun and enjoy rich foods before the fasting period of Lent. People go to fancy-dress parties and balls, dance on the streets and share delicious food.

These girls ▶ at the Venice carnival are enjoying ice-cream, a popular festival food.

Carnival in Italy has its own special food. Fried strips of pastry called *chiacchiere* are very popular in Piedmont. They are eaten dusted with icing sugar. In Sicily, children tuck into *cannoli*, sweet pastry tubes filled with sweetened cheese. People in Florence prefer *schiacciata di carnevale,* a delicious cake decorated with a chocolate lily.

▼ Some artists in Viareggio spend the whole year making floats for the carnival.

THE VIAREGGIO CARNIVAL

The carnival in the city of Viareggio has a special parade with papier-mâché statues on floats. The statues all look like famous Italian people, but they are made to look ugly. Children ride on the floats and throw confetti and sweets into the crowd.

FARINELLA

Many people at the Putignano carnival dress up as a character called Farinella. His costume is made from brightly coloured rags and his hat jingles with little bells. Farinella is named after a stew that poor farmers used to make a long time ago. It had chickpeas and barley in it.

▼ Read the recipe opposite to see how to make minestrone soup, a popular Lent dish.

Lent

The last day of carnival is called Fat Tuesday. The next day is Ash Wednesday, the beginning of Lent.

Lent lasts for forty days before Easter. Christians spend time thinking about how they can become better people. Many give up luxury foods to remember how Jesus fasted for forty days in the desert. On Fridays, they often eat meat-free meals such as minestrone soup or pasta. Some children give up sweets.

Minestrone Soup

INGREDIENTS (for 4)

- 1 Tablespoon olive oil
- 1 Small onion, finely chopped
- 1 Medium-sized potato, diced
- 1 Stalk celery, chopped
- 2 Heaped tablespoons carrots or frozen peas
- 2 Tablespoons French beans
- 50 g Pasta shapes or spaghetti
- 1 Tablespoon chopped fresh parsley or dried parsley
- 25 g Grated Parmesan cheese

EQUIPMENT

Chopping board	Electric kettle
Knife	Measuring jug
Saucepan	Ladle
Wooden spoon	

Heat the olive oil in a saucepan and cook the onions until they start to turn brown. Add the potato and celery. Cook for 6 or 7 minutes.

Slowly and carefully add half a litre of boiling water, using the measuring jug, and cook for a further 15 minutes.

Put in the rest of the vegetables and the pasta. Simmer for about 10 minutes, until the mixture is soft, but not mushy.

Stir in the parsley and the Parmesan, and serve.

Take care when you are frying and using hot liquids. Ask an adult to help.

Easter

On Good Friday, Catholics remember the day Jesus died on the cross. There are processions with people dressed as characters from the four Gospels. Men in robes carry heavy statues showing scenes from the arrest and death of Jesus. In some towns, people drag chains around their feet or hold heavy crosses. Bands play sad music.

▼ A Good Friday procession in Minori, near Naples. People wear hoods so they cannot be recognized as they ask God to forgive their sins.

◀ In Naples people make a special Easter pie called *La Pastiera*. It is filled with sweetened *ricotta* cheese, candied peel and a little orange essence.

Easter Sunday

Easter Sunday brings a change in mood. Church bells ring loudly to celebrate Christ rising from the dead. The time of fasting is over.

Many Italians have a special family dinner. In Naples, there is usually an *antipasto* of cold meats and pickled vegetables. It is followed by a special Easter *brodo* or soup, with noodles. The main course is roast lamb, served with side dishes such as fried artichokes and potatoes.

CASSATA ICE-CREAM

Cassata ice-cream was first brought to Italy by Arab cooks. Nuns copied the recipe and started making it as a special Easter treat. But in the seventeenth century they were banned by the bishop from making *cassata*. He thought they were spending too much time in the kitchen during Holy Week.

The nuns passed on the recipe to their friends and soon *cassata* was being enjoyed all over southern Italy.

Easter cakes and sweets

In northern Italy, the traditional Easter cake is shaped like a dove. It is called *colomba di Pasqua*. Some people make chocolate cherry biscuits. Others buy *schiacciata di Pasqua*, a cake made with eggs and butter. Children have chocolate Easter eggs too. The best ones come from the city of Perugia and most have a surprise toy or chocolate inside them.

▲ This Easter lamb is made from almond paste. The lamb is one of the Christian symbols for Jesus.

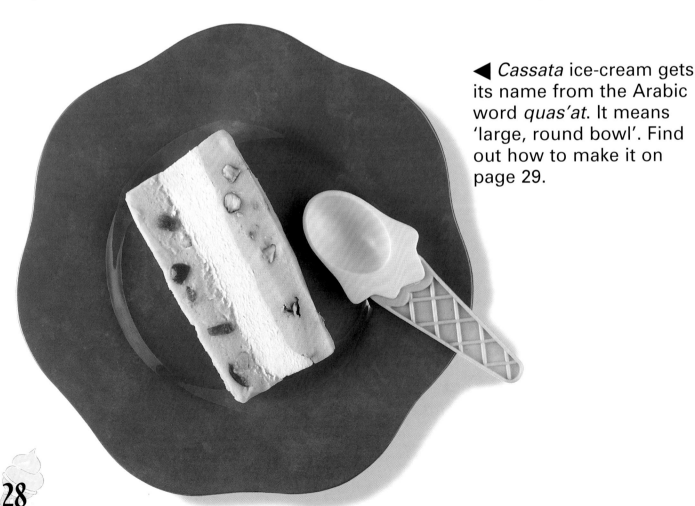

◀ *Cassata* ice-cream gets its name from the Arabic word *quas'at*. It means 'large, round bowl'. Find out how to make it on page 29.

Cassata Siciliana

INGREDIENTS (for 6)

1 large tub of vanilla ice-cream
Red food colouring
50 g Glacé cherries, chopped
50 g Candied fruit, chopped
Green food colouring
50 g Pistachio nuts

EQUIPMENT

Mixing bowl	Fork
Wooden spoon	Chopping board
Loaf tin	Knife
Cling film	

1 Allow one-third of the ice-cream to soften a little. Put in a drop of red food colouring and beat until the ice-cream turns red. Mix in the fruit.

2 Line the loaf tin with cling film. Pour in the softened ice-cream and pat into a neat layer with a wooden spoon. Return to the freezer until it hardens.

3 Soften the next third to make a white layer, returning it to the freezer in the same way. Soften the last third. Add a drop of green food colouring and mix in. Stir in the nuts and pour into the loaf tin.

4 Return the mixture to the freezer. When it has set, turn it out on to the chopping board. Cut the ice-cream neatly so that everyone gets a slice with three colours.

Always be careful with knives. Ask an adult to help you.

Glossary

Antipasto A starter course, served before the main meal.

Baptism A special ceremony for welcoming a person into the Church.

Cured Preserved by salting or smoking.

Fast To go without certain foods, or not eat at all.

Fertile Land that is good for growing crops or keeping farm animals.

Fertility Being fertile.

Gospels The first four books of the New Testament of the Bible – Matthew, Mark, Luke and John.

Holy Week The week before Easter Sunday.

Honour To show great respect for.

Liqueur A flavoured, sweetened alcoholic drink, to be drunk after a meal.

Mass A Roman Catholic service with a ceremony that celebrates Christ's death and coming to life again.

Nativity The birth of Jesus Christ.

Patron saints Saints who are seen as the special protectors of a country, church, trade or person.

Saints People whose holy deeds in life are recognized by a Church, especially the Roman Catholic Church, after they die. People honour them on special saints' days.

Photograph and artwork acknowledgements
The publishers would like to thank the following for allowing their pictures to be used in this book:
Anthony Blake Photo Library 14, 16 (above), (Tim Imrie) 27, (John Sims) 28 (above); Britstock (Eric Bach) 9, (Tschanz) 11; Cephas (Franck Auberson) 22 (left); Getty Images (Chris Windsor) *cover photo*, (Andy Sacks) 6; Chapel Studios (Alistair Beckett) 7 and 10, (Zul Mukhida) 16 (below), 20, 24 and 28 (below); Food Features 19; Robert Harding (John G. Ross) 18 (right), (Mike Newton) 26; Hutchison (Nancy Durrell-McKenna) 5 (bottom left), (Robert Aberman) 8 (both), (Gail Goodger) 18 (left); Norma Joseph 13, 22 (right); Kronos 2000 15; Pictor International 12, 23; Wayland Picture Library 5 (top right).

While every effort has been made to trace copyright holders, in one case this has not proved possible.

Fruit and vegetable artwork is by Tina Barber. The map artwork on page 4 is by Peter Bull and Hardlines. The step-by-step recipe artwork is by Judy Stevens.

Topic Web and Resources

MATHS
Using and understanding data and measures (recipes).

Using and reading measuring instruments: scales.

Using weights and measures.

Using and understanding fractions.

SCIENCE
Food and nutrition.

Health.

Plants in different habitats.

Plants as a life process.

Mixing and dissolving different materials.

Changing materials through heat.

GEOGRAPHY
Locality study.

Landscapes and climate.

Farming.

Influence of landscape on human activities: farming and food festivals.

Awareness of wider context of a place.

DESIGN AND TECHNOLOGY
Design a poster to advertise a food product.

Technology used in food production.

Food preparation.

Follow a recipe.

Food & Festivals
TOPIC WEB

HISTORY
British food today: where did it come from and how?

Investigate the different farming methods used over the past century.

MODERN FOREIGN LANGUAGES
Language skills.

Everyday activities: food.

People, places and customs.

MUSIC
As part of celebration.

Music from a different culture.

ENGLISH
Make up a slogan to sell a food product.

Write a poem or story using food as the subject.

Write a menu for a lavish Italian meal.

R.E.
Food and festivals.

Christianity:

Christmas, Epiphany, Lent, Easter, baptism, weddings.

OTHER BOOKS TO READ

Celebration! by Barnabas and Annabel Kindersley (Dorling Kindersley, 1997)

Christmas by Clare Chandler (Wayland, 1996)

Country Topics: Italy by R. Wright (Franklin Watts, 1994)

Easter by Philip Sauvain (Wayland, 1997)

Focus on Italy and the Italians by Ed Meedham (Franklin Watts, 1994)

Get Set, Go: Spring Festivals by H. Bliss (Franklin Watts, 1995)

Look Inside Italy by Joy Richardson (Franklin Watts, 1995)

Pasta by Jillian Powell (Wayland, 1996)

This book meets the following specific objectives of the National Literacy Strategy's Framework for Teaching:

✔ Range of work in non-fiction: simple recipes (especially Year 2, Term 1), instructions, labels, captions, lists, glossary, index.

✔ Vocabulary extension: words linked to particular topics (food words) and technical words from work in other subjects (geography and food science).

Index

Page numbers in **bold** mean there is a photograph on the page.

Topic Web and Resources

MATHS

Using and understanding data and measures (recipes).

Using and reading measuring instruments: scales.

Using weights and measures.

Using and understanding fractions.

SCIENCE

Food and nutrition.

Health.

Plants in different habitats.

Plants as a life process.

Mixing and dissolving different materials.

Changing materials through heat.

GEOGRAPHY

Locality study.

Landscapes and climate.

Farming.

Influence of landscape on human activities: farming and food festivals.

Awareness of wider context of a place.

DESIGN AND TECHNOLOGY

Design a poster to advertise a food product.

Technology used in food production.

Food preparation.

Follow a recipe.

Food & Festivals
TOPIC WEB

HISTORY

British food today: where did it come from and how?

Investigate the different farming methods used over the past century.

MODERN FOREIGN LANGUAGES

Language skills.

Everyday activities: food.

People, places and customs.

MUSIC

As part of celebration.

Music from a different culture.

ENGLISH

Make up a slogan to sell a food product.

Write a poem or story using food as the subject.

Write a menu for a lavish Italian meal.

R.E.

Food and festivals.

Christianity:

Christmas, Epiphany, Lent, Easter, baptism, weddings.

OTHER BOOKS TO READ

Celebration! by Barnabas and Annabel Kindersley (Dorling Kindersley, 1997)

Christmas by Clare Chandler (Wayland, 1996)

Country Topics: Italy by R. Wright (Franklin Watts, 1994)

Easter by Philip Sauvain (Wayland, 1997)

Focus on Italy and the Italians by Ed Meedham (Franklin Watts, 1994)

Get Set, Go: Spring Festivals by H. Bliss (Franklin Watts, 1995)

Look Inside Italy by Joy Richardson (Franklin Watts, 1995)

Pasta by Jillian Powell (Wayland, 1996)

This book meets the following specific objectives of the National Literacy Strategy's Framework for Teaching:

✓ Range of work in non-fiction: simple recipes (especially Year 2, Term 1), instructions, labels, captions, lists, glossary, index.

✓ Vocabulary extension: words linked to particular topics (food words) and technical words from work in other subjects (geography and food science).

Index

Page numbers in **bold** mean there is a photograph on the page.